SEASONS OF FUN: SPRING

SPRING PLANTS

by J. P. Press

Consultant: Beth Gambro
Reading Specialist, Yorkville, Illinois

Minneapolis, Minnesota

Teaching Tips

Before Reading

- Look at the cover of the book. Discuss the picture and the title.
- Ask readers to brainstorm a list of what they already know about plants in the spring. What can they expect to see in the book?
- Go on a picture walk, looking through the pictures to discuss vocabulary and make predictions about the text.

During Reading

- Read for purpose. Encourage readers to think about what happens to plants in the spring as they are reading.
- Ask readers to look for the details of the book. What is happening?
- If readers encounter an unknown word, ask them to look at the sounds in the word. Then, ask them to look at the rest of the page. Are there any clues to help them understand?

After Reading

- Encourage readers to pick a buddy and reread the book together.
- Ask readers to name three things from the book that happen to spring plants. Go back and find the pages that tell about these things.
- Ask readers to write or draw something they learned about spring plants.

Credits:
Cover and title page, © LiliGraphie/Shutterstock; 3, © OllyLo/Shutterstock; 5, © tividan/Shutterstock; 7, © emholk/iStock; 8–9, © DiyanaDimitrova/iStock; 11, © birdpits/Shutterstock; 12–13, © JacobH/iStock; 15, © Singkham/Shutterstock; 16–17, © valio84sl/iStock; 17, © Zoran Zeremski/iStock; 19, © M_Agency/Shutterstock; 21, © Darren Baker/Shutterstock; 22, © Александр Довянский/iStock; © cobalt88/Shutterstock; 23TL, © Kristyna Henkeova/Shutterstock; 23TM, © Africa Studio/Shutterstock; 23TR, © Chutharat Kamkhuntee/Shutterstock; 23BL, © Sergiy Bykhunenko/Shutterstock; 23BM, -© lovelyday12/iStock; 23BR, © Allexxandar/iStock.

Library of Congress Cataloging-in-Publication Data

Names: Press, J. P., 1993- author.
Title: Spring plants / J.P. Press ; consultant: Beth Gambro, Reading
Specialist, Yorkville, Illinois
Description: Bearcub books. | Minneapolis : Bearport Publishing Company,
[2022] | Series: Seasons of fun : spring | Includes bibliographical
references and index.
Identifiers: LCCN 2021030927 (print) | LCCN 2021030928 (ebook) | ISBN
9781636913964 (library binding) | ISBN 9781636914015 (paperback) | ISBN
9781636914060 (ebook)
Subjects: LCSH: Spring plants--Juvenile literature. | Plants--Juvenile
literature. | Spring--Juvenile literature.
Classification: LCC QK49 .P74 2022 (print) | LCC QK49 (ebook) | DDC
580--dc23
LC record available at https://lccn.loc.gov/2021030927
LC ebook record available at https://lccn.loc
.gov/2021030928

For more information, write to Bearport Publishing, 5357 Penn Avenue South, Minneapolis, MN 55419.
Printed in the United States of America.

Contents

Time to Grow

It is time for spring fun!

Spring brings new plant life.

Let's watch the plants grow!

The weather gets warmer when winter ends.

Rain **melts** the last of the snow.

The water will help spring plants grow.

So will the sun.

When the ground warms up, plants can grow.

Small green **shoots** pop out of the dirt.

A shoot

The green shoots get taller.
Soon, they grow leaves.
Their flowers **bloom**.

Other plants start growing, too.

Trees and bushes get new leaves.

There are more and more flowers.

Spring is full of color!

Some plants grow in the same spot every year.

They stay under the ground during winter.

Then, they come up in the spring.

Other plants must be **planted** each year.

Farmers start planting in the spring.

They put seeds in the ground to grow food.

Plants grown for food are called **crops**.

Farmers water their crops.

They keep bugs away from the plants, too.

In a few months, the crops will be ready to eat!

Some spring flowers only stay for a short time.

Other plants keep growing until fall or winter.

We will see all the plants again next spring!

How Plants Grow

Many plants start as seeds or **bulbs**. They are planted under the ground.

Soon, roots reach down into the dirt. Shoots poke up out of the dirt.

The shoots grow bigger. Sun and water help the plants grow.

As plants get bigger, they may start to have leaves. Some grow flowers.

Glossary

bloom to open as a flower

bulbs parts of plants that are under the ground

crops plants that are grown for food

melts turns from solid to liquid

planted set in the ground as a seed or bulb that will grow

shoots young plants that have just come out of the ground

Index

Read More

Fraser, Finley. *Harvest (Seasons of Fun: Fall).* Minneapolis: Bearport Publishing, 2021.

Gaertner, Meg. *Spring Plants (Spring Is Here).* Lake Elmo, MN: Focus Readers, 2020.

Learn More Online

1. Go to **www.factsurfer.com** or scan the QR code below.
2. Enter "**Spring Plants**" into the search box.
3. Click on the cover of this book to see a list of websites.

About the Author

J. P. Press likes reading books and watching things grow.